Candlefish

POEMS BY
ELIZABETH BILLER CHAPMAN

The University of Arkansas Press
Fayetteville
2004

08 07 06 05 04   5 4 3 2 1

Designed by Liz Lester

⊗ The paper used in this publication meets the minimum require-
ments of the American National Standard for Permanence of Paper
for Printed Library Materials Z39.48-1984.

LIBRARY OF CONGRESS CATALOGING-IN-PUBLICATION DATA

Chapman, Elizabeth Biller, 1943–
Candlefish : poems / by Elizabeth Biller Chapman.
p.   cm.
ISBN 1-55728-767-8 (pbk. : alk. paper)
I. Title.
PS3603.H365C36   2004
811'.54—dc22   2003020530

For Sylvia Burack
in memory

ACKNOWLEDGMENTS

Grateful acknowledgment is made to the following publications, in which these poems have appeared.

American Tanka: "February"; *Bellowing Ark:* "Waking to the Early Trees," "Windfall," "For My Mother's Eightieth Birthday," "Of Fates and Fireweed," "Candlefish," "Dream of My Father Walking Toward Me," "By Moody Marsh," "Light Arriving (The Strait of Georgia)"; *Blueline:* "I Remember That Green Day," "Cosmos"; *Blue Unicorn:* "Neither Can the Floods Drown It"; *California State Poetry Society Quarterly (CQ):* "Amber"; *The Comstock Review:* "The Bird Hide," "Feast of Stephen," "What Happens in Spring Rain"; *Green Mountains Review (GMR):* "Papermill Creek"; *Manzanita Quarterly:* "Everywhere I Feel the Stars of Fall," "Sleeping with Cedar," "Little Black Rails," "In Greenmeadow with Helen, Walking the Dog," "Summer Vespers, Bel Canto," "The Feast Day of St. Francis"; *Poetry:* "Liking Men, Mistress Quickly," "In Kona, Thinking of the Elements"; *Potato Eyes:* "Owling in the Arroyo Hondo, a Song for the Fall Equinox"; *Prairie Schooner:* "Adobe"; *Smith Voices* (anthology, ed. Patricia Skarda, The Smith College Press, 1999): "It Snowed"; *Sow's Ear Poetry Review:* "Mockingbird, Fulton Street"; *The Texas Observer:* "This Rueful Moon."

CONTENTS

NOTE ON CANDLEFISH

English name for oolichan or eulichon (fr. Chinook), a marine
fish, *Thaleichthys pacificus,* native to the Pacific Northwest and
British Columbia, renowned as a source of food and especially
—due to its high oil content—light; "so oily that when dried
it may be used as a candle by drawing a wick through it"
(Webster, 2nd ed., unabridged). Cf. also A. Ross, *Adventures,
First Settlers, Oregon River* (1849): "There is a small fish resem-
bling the smelt or herring, known by the name of ulichon,
which enters the river in immense shoals in the spring of the
year"; and J. G. Frazer, *Golden Bough: Magic Art* (1911): "The
Indians of British Columbia believe that twins can . . . call
[forth] salmon and the oolachen or candle-fish."

Candlefish

1

Thinning the apples
    to twosomes, a sack in one hand,
        I twist off the hard green knobs, telling by the feel
           of cluster and stem, which are frailer.

If this is what the Bible calls dominion, it's
    a little sad; I look for signs of fruitfulness
        beyond these trees—a grapevine
           no one can account for, by the sunroom here.

Nature is prolific: My father's voice—
    Twenty years dead this last Sunday; and my mother fell,
        a bad bruise. How soon till
           he'll gather her in?

Covering the storage box
    morning-glories open, a few cups of summer sky.

2

Portia, sleek chestnut, true to her tribe,
    shows some white of eye when I enter.
        She's known to shy at pigeons,
           quicken her pace with the wind.

We practice crossovers. Her legs braid beneath me,
　　then we serpentine through the big arena. My shoulders
　　　　swivel to match her ears. I have to keep the bearing
　　　　　　　　　　　　rein
　　　　steady at the withers—bending her—

and remember to breathe through
　　the transitions, all at once thinking of a singular day,
　　　　　　　　　　very hot:
　　at St. John's Hospital, the clock at one-oh-four,
　　　　　　　　　　　the doctor saying
　　　　A beautiful girl. Turned twenty-five a week ago.

The mare trots a circle—so relaxed
　　my eyes can close. Later, standing to be rubbed
　　　　she glistens, bathed in many lights.

　　3
And still amid the alien corn, Ruth weeps.
　　Only in nature can we eat
　　　　the half-forgotten grain
　　　　　　of Paradise.

4

Have you heard of the oolichan? Those sea fish crammed
                                        with oil.
    Every spring, huge shoals of them raked into Tsimshian
                                        canoes,
        dried, threaded with a wick, stuck in the sand—
                                        and lit,
            each one becoming incandescent, a candle.

Connecting, we ignite: a shift of the tide, a balm.
    Look down, my lovely daughter, can you see?
        The floor of our house is glass, and the candlefish
                                        are swimming there.
            Over and over it happens—

The day draws on; the apples ripen
    toward the Angelus hour. Tired out,
        his face shaded by an old cap,
            my father naps on a hammock in the garden.

Now, the bit removed, her stall set fair,
    sweet Portia dozes—
        rye-grass piled around her feet.

Summer Vespers, Bel Canto

Topaz, the last light gathers like smoke above the dark
hills curving west to the fire lookout and departs,

a spirit taking leave of its body, ridge by ridge.
All week we've kept watch over this valley and our flock,

"Los Carpinteros"—acorn woodpeckers who racket
and hammer through the oaks and on our roof beam, *Wake*-up,

Wake-up—and a sprout of moon rises at their knocking.

This is a rough landscape, long known to you. A dreamy
brush rabbit stirs but does not budge from the still-warm path.

The fog's gray wool folds back westward to the outer bay.
Trawling, the jellies pulse their bells—Lion's Mane, Crystal,

Sea-Nettle, Lobed Comb, Gooseberry—all those old selves
tumbling together in the open water, dying

into each other's lives. Now my home is where you are.
At your brother Ned's house in the next draw, yielding up

her heart, Janet Baker sings Berlioz, *Summer Nights,*
that mezzo soprano surrounding us like July dusk,

these shadows. Fiercely green, the wild oak leaves arc upward.

Adobe

For Helen Stepanov

*Shall I not have intelligence with the
earth? Am I not partly leaves and
vegetable mould, myself?*

HENRY THOREAU, *WALDEN*

I

Her eyes are dark almonds, remembering
summers on the Baltic, the beaches smooth
underfoot, scuffing up pieces of amber
scalloped on one side by the sea.

We have had our iced tea and applesauce
at a picnic table in the small state park.
Michael, ten, and Peter, eleven, are chasing a hen
around the old settlers' cabin.

*That was Lithuania, then.
Even the cemetery was beautiful. We would go
walking there. I was never scared.*

She tugs at her cotton T-shirt.
Breast, ribs and shoulder—the whole right side—are in flames.
Monday the injections will begin.

It will take a year. *A one in two chance,*
she'd told me on the phone.
Will you come with us Friday, to San Juan Bautista?
I'd like to visit the Mission again.

2

Halfway down the long nave, bear tracks
have imprinted the old tile, its clear red
pulling us. Two converts, we kneel at the rail.
You're younger than I—and more strict.

Today we bend the rules: "No Childrens."
Your sons drop in their quarters. Bluely
their votives blaze upward to the slight statue, her dress ecru,
Our Lady, acquainted with loss.

The padres knew how to pick a site.
Out the north door, the graveyard, olive trees showering
their silver. Below this hilltop, farms extend:
ripe fields of garlic, ordinary corn.

In the fathers' garden, your face
brightens at a clump of blossoms
the scarlet of fine raspberry jam.

Asters. In Russia we thought of them as
fall flowers. Red-dipped finches hover
in this beseeching air like angels.

3

At the old stable, a stuffed cougar snarls from the wall
and a sign for stagecoach travelers cries, "Woe"
with the voice of Jeremiah: Expect
Annoyances. Cold. Abundant Dust.

What can I do? Helen says. *It's the truth.*
Peter came with me to see
the video, how they will tattoo my breast, before . . .

Let's take some pictures now. With hair.
We pose in different combinations on a grassy spot
between a sundial and a chestnut rose.
The drowsy petals smell a lot like tea.

Michael—once a towhead, now dark blond
and blue-eyed like his father—
gestures at a pile of weathered brick. "It's mud,
with hay in it. They put it in the sun to dry. Adobe."

We nectar on this day somehow, like
brush-foot butterflies—my friend, a Lorquin's Admiral, fire
hedging the tip of each black upper wing.

4

Two days after tomorrow, the nurse
will lay a heating pad on your arm

to bring up the veins, drip in medicine for nausea,
then push: two plungers of thick poison.

It will take three hours. Your veins will resist.
You will feel very tired and ill.
Your heart muscle may weaken.

5
Still, there are deliverances:
Just this morning when I was finishing my walk
at Garland Ranch, a middle-aged horsewoman asked
"Are you crossing the bridge?"
and said, "He will find the courage to follow you."
As the tall bay thoroughbred was stepping after me
over a mild Carmel River, I heard the story—
six years old, given her off the track,
his left front cannon bone fractured, sterile by then,
        from steroids.
"I've had him gelded, hope
to turn him into a trail horse. His racing name
was 'Ask Me.' I call him 'Joy.'"
She clucked. He picked up the trot.
They passed me on the riverbank
disappearing among willows.

6

Yet I believe you will return
from exile, like the basket of good figs in the Bible:
And none shall be missing.

We'll be sipping tea from glasses
like our Polish-speaking grandmothers. You will mix
idioms, the way I love:
One of a sudden . . .

That's quick,
quick as the snapdragon yawn of a cat.
Your eyes will hold mine:
So, you will ask, *How is your life?*

Papermill Creek

At swim in the heron's pasture
mauve pennyroyal at the edge
where I undress My feet bruise it
releasing a frank scent the last
day of my fifty-fourth year

A local benefaction
this water rushing green-white through
the sluice and pausing pooling
and shoaling here I strike out
modestly still in my long shirt

How avidly we try to grasp
what's leaving us the sunflower all
center that gold wilted or gone
He's waiting now among the reeds
stock-still one great blue heron

Time is riparian this hour
a sparrow briefly caught
between two fingers a whirring heart
and clasping my knuckle the twigs
of her legs their fragile claws

Mockingbird, Fulton Street

His voice is leaves.
He is singing out,
pouring his liquid names on the night

as you sleep beside me.
You are better at peacefulness and sleep than I.

Coming in from my walk today,
I found on the floor of the porch your iris teacup
and napkin and book, Stafford's *Scripture of Leaves*,
to carry inside. Walking's so difficult for you

you stay in each place a long time now,
anchoring like a seahorse, upright on his blade
of ocean grass. Reliable.

"It is a fearful thing to love
What Death can touch."

My father kept that inscription
from a New Hampshire graveyard in his wallet,
where we stumbled on it after he died.

In the garden—it is early May—
our hydrangea breaks

her tight green bonds, bursting into white
ascension. The light is everything.

"I love you," I say, "Promise to care for you, Promise
to go on writing."

Under a mother's moon
the mockingbird notes fly out
ascending, a voice of leaves.

In Kona, Thinking of the Elements

The Trades: After midnight they grow strong as the surf,
rattle the palms' green teeth, entice them to drop
their coconut riches. A few fall smooth, hairless and unripe.

Springtime, my first morning back, and five Nene geese
peck about the roots of a *hau* thicket, send their
muted cry seaward, "Who, you?" Darkness furrows each neck.

Always in Kona I think of the elements. By the road
bending through lava, a donkey grazes on small plants;
his body's the color of this black, volcanic earth.

A slatch of the wind, a calm behind big waves, breaking—
here, over finger and lobe, the names of fish swim in:
Yellow Tang, Pinktail, Moorish Idol, Lemon Butterfly.

Time and Desire become one dream: the oldest planet,
                                circling
our heavens, and the parrotfish, grinding coral to make sand.
Two sea turtles sprawl on the beach at four as if blown there.

The *hau* trees live long; they thrive on the seepage of salt.
What if rancor and sorrow would, like the *hau* blossom,
wither in a single day? each flower gliding, yellow

to mango then flaming deeper orange to red as
the coin of this realm, the sun. What if this were how life's
afternoon slipped down, extravagant into evening?

Dream of My Father Walking Toward Me

After breakfast—his egg, poached; toast; the Boston *Herald*
folded and obituaries always read—he comes
stepping right out in the sharp morning scent of after-shave.

Rain, and a south wind
beguiling our quinces
into flower, my mind's across the country.

What's haunting my mother
in deep winter, in the small hours

(I cannot know) is not
my business to transact,
but something just now is being sold.

And I remember (my father's hand nicely warm)
going along Commonwealth, the Mall and city birds;
up brownstone steps; the switchboard operator (her worn
            smile,
her hair tidied at the neck) plugged in each call.

The elevator still had shined brass trim.
Upstairs smelled of rubber cement and the girls' perfume.
Black Royal typewriters, clacking,
and a quaint address-o-graph.

Last month he would have turned ninety-two.

Late bulbs are going into the ground today:
allium, anemone, narcissus. Leaf tips
like green nipples push through paper skin.

Daily, the documents arrive.
One willow in the Public Garden grieves.
I remember he loved his work,
and him telling me, *Look for people who are kind.*

I didn't always listen.

    Dark shapes flash before my eyes—
    time to prune what's dormant, to discuss which trees
    are likely to bear fruit. I look for ways
    to clip the downward growing stems.

Deep winter and old night,
I look for him,
my father walking toward me

In the kitchen window
when the morning light is strong,
you can discern (within its bud)

the flower's form,
a branched shadow that will split its sheath
opening the podded life.

Rain's dampening the bulbs now gone into the earth.
And our white quince is in flower.

For My Mother's Eighteenth Birthday

1

The day's first fragrance: Narcissus lean at a fragile
angle from their porcelain bowl
into the room with the pullout bed.
Outside, chickadees take breakfast from the feeder crammed
with black-oil sunflower seed, while squirrels
watch from a hemlock trunk, brushy tails aloft.

On our walk to Lost Pond, we gather a few berries,
two red oak leaves, dead loosestrife like feathers
of straw. My longtime friend mentions her father,
who dwindles in a nursing home. What to do
with his ashes? The sky unpacks its gray wool
in strands, this rain falling, silver yarn binding us.

2

Seventy-two Penniman Road—
through the kitchen window, the same
thermometer, its large red dial
showing thirty-six degrees at noon.
Abbey, the Irish housekeeper,
fixes macaroni and cheese.

Twenty-three years ago she rocked my infant daughter,
Katie, in the laundry basket

singing, *Seesaw, Margery Daw,*
Jacky shall have a new master.
Several hours before the party
we're carried by that current, still.

   3

Arriving in sleet, the guests shed
their heavy coats and are fed cream of butternut squash.
At the last minute I'm writing my speech:
at North Station, about to board the camp train, the lunch
I'd forgotten, replaced, without blaming. My mother's
generosity of spirit.

The slides follow one another: My father is here.
Abe marries Sylvia, her plum velvet
lifting on a swirl of Sinatra music. Three girls born
and—their faces a winter bouquet—grandchildren, all nine.
We will think of this night—its rich palette of carmine,
gold, ultramarine—with joy.

As when in a storm, you and I
listen to the creek rise and boil
and divine that the floodgate will hold, and retire—
(the cats' faces against our green
blanket like two wedges of pie)
for once content to inhabit this body, this house.

February

Month with no full moon—
the swale gloom deepens. I stroke
pale ears of catkins.
Colors race through willow stems:
copper, cloth-of-gold, daybreak.

My footsteps lengthen
in the spaces between trees—
particles of cloud,
blackberry ravens calling,
Listen. Winter is going.

Neither Can the Floods Drown It

For M.

We catch only glimpses of you,
my twenty-one-year-old, my wildcat
daughter disappearing through
underbrush and shadow
as you struggle to become.

In the years of *otitis media,*
I worried myself sick about your ears.
Healed now, keen as anyone's,
they'll pick up a whisper,
your name three rooms away.

Lynx, a word for you, means
quickness of sight,
your eyes hazel-green always noticing
when the sad vases were empty,
each parrot tulip stripe, each pairing

of pistil with stamen
when they were full. Know this:
you have left tracks—those pastels you loved,
mother-of-pearl and alabaster
Caran d'Ache. Tones of earth and fire,

I can see you still—
tawny hair, that walk with toes turned out,
padding under the loquat's leathery rain,
leftward into what was and will be
your green world.

What Happens in Spring Rain

Grass, like green fire, lifts
her inward heat from the earth,
high enough to scythe.
A nighthawk circles our slope.
He is a wave. I'm planting

Rock-Rose and Fragrant
Plum. My daughters dream of names,
infants sprinkling their
future. Day and season float:
a heart shape, a mock-orange leaf.

Kneedeep, I'm hearing

Kneedeep, the bullfrogs

from winter mud, pulse
upward to couple and dunk,
each throat puffing out
yellow-green as the iris
blossom kneedeep all around

this reflecting pond.

knew what her pleasures were a posset
    and a sea-coal fire her knight at her
side Can it be thirty-five years since
    a nineteen-year-old waif with guitar
arriving in Stratford fell promptly
    (in love) from his wineglass the dark stain
yet marking my *Four Quartets* In our
    tavern The Windmill a parrot screeched
Act Four in the paddock nothing but
    lusty grass prickling I leapt a wall
and there at New Place hearing my first
    Myfanwy (beloved) I half swooned
Nights now when my husband's leg goes numb
    and cold I feel under the bedclothes
remember *Dust thou art and to dust*
    we will become and put out my hand
like a mussel's holdfast organ of
    attaching to a rock latching on
In the slow sea-current this neap tide
    nibbling the Crow Moon's edge (into Spring)
we mingle in the gentlest of all
    water till (no more sighing and grief)
morning dips her beak in the March sun
    mist rising from our shingles like breath

Cosmos

How, on the border of Fall,
they radiate through my Bolinas garden—
how the butterflies love these purple blossoms,
climbing their robust stalks
like the angels on Jacob's ladder.
How these faces, mauve and rose
and ripest crabapple, hold us
for this moment in September.

What is the wingspan of pelicans,
four or five feet?

As the sun sinks, you and I
watch them sail on a high wind,
fourteen brown S-shapes
faithful to this corner of the ocean.
We make room for them,
for the tide of feeling
the long of you
against the bracelets of my wrists,
in the trenches of my palms.

Did you know that the tops of clouds
are called anvils?

At night
they ring us down the avenues of sleep
where we walk in the old
garden of the body—
pine tree and stone wall and roses
out of the ground like a fountain—
the body, the cosmos, whose radiance
binds us, compelling as blood.

Everywhere I Feel the Stars of Fall

They engrave the dark.
When the moon is new, an equinoctial tide
lifts the nests of harvest mice. At dusk

the Great Bear hugs the horizon
while I ride the new mare into Purisima Gorge.
Her coat's the color of madrone bark.

We sway with each change in the wind.
She flicks her ears. I stroke the long red hill of her neck:
Lady Pegasus, with scratches.

The crickets' song grows faint.
Above me, Cassiopeia's butterfly floats
from her hook of eternity,

and all around, forever in their gauzy net,
Night's tears, the dimmer stars of autumn, etch
the dark, expanding in us here.

Owling in the Arroyo Hondo,
a Song for the Fall Equinox

I

Large as a cat on the cypress-snag, and solid,
turning his head from side to side
he looks half asleep until he hears us
and moves to a more distant tree—
that fine gray barring visible from below
but not his feathered eyelids.
I can imagine them
and the wing-ends fringed like a prayer shawl.

Later, surprised by moonlight,
he'll hoot for hours
about life by the arroyo, the deep stream
rising and falling, the smaller birds
growing restless—warblers, vireos,
the kinglets with their high tinkling—
how they practice every evening, hopping, facing south,
then lifting through the cloud of alder green,
how, finally, they leave him.

"I have always," says this moon of dying grass
and harvest, "loved one great horned owl best."

2

Walking from Heart's Desire
to Indian Beach, I put my feet in Tomales Bay,
wading around the moon jellies flopped on the sand,
their transparent lives outgrown.

The sound of gulls and the tide seem as usual.
An egret preens his plumes.
Curved like eyebrows, harbor seals warm
pale bellies in September sun.

Still, the bishop pines—corrugated,
a hand-span between their creases—
must sense what's coming on: autumn, that sadness
which lies beneath all passion.
I wonder if they feel uncovered, as I do.

3

The last shall be first,
our gospel for today,
a Sunday in ordinary time.

In our kitchen the light's like green tea
steeping in a glass mug,
or russet-apple skin.

I've scrambled eggs the Irish way,
warming milk with the butter, and we eat them
with tomatoes from the garden.

On the table sits a candle, unlit,
the color of honey, the shape
of a bee skep, or a breast.

Married nine months,
harvesting, you claim a kiss. Eleven in the morning
as summer softly goes to sleep.

The Feast Day of St. Francis

The year bends the air thistle-dry
    overripe this morning A sparrow hawk
        alights on a parched
            cornstalk in the creek-side garden its old
                grape-stake gate sprung open

and pumps her tail
    the blend of tawny and dark
        like those still tasseled remains
            after harvest Dahlias drowse
                purple and the scarecrow stares

Rounding the corner there I feel
    the equinoctial light
        narrowed in the kestrel's eye
            Packed rod and cone reflect a cricket shape
                or ultraviolet trace of vole

The world curves the downward
    floating of leaf spiraled
        muscle around bone Creeks
            wind through our clay Soon the wild
                bird will stoop and be gone

Animals have souls And sublunary they die
 yet are saved inside us carried
  the way the moon's half circle holds
   a rabbit or that bluish sea whose pale blood
    spilled earlier by skylight on my kitchen floor

Mare Fecunditatis Our fig tree
 now drips milk where each fruit falls
  or is plucked Two cats a calico
   a tortoise sniff that ground and roll
    brindled like October earth

Sleeping with Cedar

The click of toenails, some clawing,
and she has jumped up on the quilt

to lie beside me. Her face is lined
like her St. Bernard grandmother's.

Through the maple tree, already
maroon and rust, the first rain

has been falling all afternoon
on Ganges harbor, on the street-

market where an old man's beetroot
swim in their washtub like red trout.

In my attic room with a wide
brass bed, she's found me. Cedar, whose

fur looks, even smells, like sweet wood.
She burrows closer, and we doze

like litter mates in natal darkness.
The sunlight has curled up, to wait.

Flowers turned to down,
the golden-bush goes off in whiskery seed.

Of Fates and Fireweed

I

I am a guest here.

From this cottage window, I can see
November arrive—a red shovel, leaning
near a stripe of earth already turned
for winter planting.
Among disconsolate marrows, crows
ignore the clothed effigy, glean
what they can and fly off. Their feet
rotate, like oars feathering
so the wind slips by.

Tomorrow's the Day of the Dead.
Arbutus weeps her berries on the beach.
The long limbs of these strawberry trees
grow as we do; their skin peels.
I am shown what's left of the Tsaout:
clamshells, and one carving
the sea fills and refills—that bowl
for greeting salmon
is perfect. Reflects the moon.

2

November second: Rushing to the ferry, we stop
at the sign, High Mountain Honey.
Jars piled on a cedar cream-stand, dark and light.
I choose the palest, nearly as clear as water.
That's pearly and fireweed. The apiarist will not

let me go, describing his bee yard across the strait,
its utter, flower-scented happiness, then Fall—
the hives' night-traveling back to Salt Spring,
this farmland which he calls The Valley of the Bees.
Wait. Take this label. Some postcards. Here. His eyes are wild.

3

How unmistakable, our naming,
the anthropology of love. Driving south

I am thinking about words, myself half-mad with them.
They are my bees, a tribe
feeding on the smoke-hot, purple air, fanning their wings
to concentrate the nectar more.
It dishevels me to conjure up that sonorous place
where it is always All Souls—a gate
swung open—and always August,
an essence to distill even now, as

high in the Sooke Hills, the fireweed and pearly everlasting
sleep, beneath new frost, their vegetable sleep.

By Moody Marsh

Forsan et haec olim meminisse juvabit.

VIRGIL, *AENEID*

Gulls wheel.
I extract the wretched cat and carry her—
swaddled, the towel damp with pee—
lurching over crushed shells to a bench.
The air is clean
and, with soothing nonsense, I rock her,
　　Tabby, nearly twenty,
　　my *gatita anciana,*

　　What is the word for this water?

A standing tide—
I become idly aware of splashes, a small
hummock there on the channel,
one pintail's umber brown
upending when he dives.
From Pothole Country far beyond the Rockies,
they winter here.

Only the cat's head shows. I turn
so what sun there is can lay its hand on her.
And Tabby extends a ginger neck,

resting her larynx quiet against my fleece.
It is Advent Sunday: Isaiah's
>   *We have all withered like leaves,*
>   *our guilt carries us away.*

The breeze is sweet.

We have
a few more minutes, a mackerel sky, its gray
now suffused with yellow. This time,
like that engraving I love—*Folding the Last Sheep*—
outlines each eyelid, the white
grass of whiskers.
Our faces, marked with parting light.

Some day even this will please us to remember.

"Guadalupe Days"

Scrunched there, mind on the river, the heron knows
its slow truckle, knows each morning is holy:
a young nun selling candied *guayaba;* those
children eating their first bread of heaven;
the pelican begging for a gobbet, *Ten
Piedad, Señor,* his pouch pink-wet inside.

Above them flies the frigate bird like a dark
shuttle, threading his thousand furlongs of sky.

Fresh tides wash the *malecón.* December, street-
drums for the virgin whose soul doth magnify—
the surf's great bell, crashing on iron-red rock:
Word, made flesh. Before the angel of the Lord
disclosed to Mary, might she have heard this wind,
rising, lift the fragile garment of her sleep?

In Greenmeadow with Helen, Walking the Dog

Hunting, Dylan puts his nose to the ground.
His behind wiggles, sending a squirrel
up a camphor tree. *He needs grass,* you say,

so we follow those short, Welsh Corgi legs
around the sand track, again and again.

It is a day of sharp focus. What leaves
are left, stand out after violent rain.

The catheter's in place: Tomorrow you'll
enter Stanford Hospital. They'll implant your own stem cells,
the old bone marrow killed.

Only in times of peace can we afford
symmetry, said Klee of his *Angel, Still
Feminine*—her flamed breasts tucked in one wing.

I've grown used to your skullcap and loose shirt.
We talk of women's things: the children, church.

It almost doesn't matter. Cold and clear,
this three o'clock, this crape myrtle's red, edged

with black. Your young cattle dog, doing just
what he's been bred to do, herding the kids
home from school. His eyes darken with purpose.

Windfall

A letter to my daughters

Dear Katie and Maggie,

Again it is storming outside. I waked remembering—
west of here, this afternoon,
my friend will breed her white Arabian,
Shatana, for the first time.
A light's been burning in her stall
night and day all this month past,
an encouragement to catch. As if it were—
February were—Spring.

I do envy that mare. Not
Mr. Ego, the dusky stallion
covering her sound back end
but afterward, those gradual mysteries:
gestation, round and rounder, the extra grain;
then lactating, the milk
tinged with madness and wonder;
that year spent giving suck.

All afternoon, they've been winching dead trees from the creek.
The whine of it. The grappling hook.

Did you know? Two owls were mating last night
(hey, ho, the wind and the rain).
Could you hear them, all the way to the city
where you live?

Windfall:
Adjective applied to
a flood of unexpected light.
My dictionary says you are my windfall
daughters. When you call (mostly) or visit,
a shaft of it—light—crosses my winter week,
brightens it, like a branch of our white
flowering quince in blossom.

Saturday it was boxes, PRIVATE CONSTELLATIONS.
Wood, reflecting glass and glue.
Katie, you
brought me to Joseph Cornell, *Crow Song in Orion,*
The Rain Barrel, with rabbit and plumy carrot, not far from
when you were four, your whole room spun with yarn:
Katie's web. My mother, wanting to snip
(dangerous). Sacred objects dangled there,
a maze of colors. A Naiad, you swam your way through.

"I'm sick of being the perfect daughter."
Now you want to quit your bank job,
go to the Academy full time,

learn to make films.
Move to a cheaper place (a loft, with a Murphy bed?).
Wonderful. We saw that exhibit on the 31st,
which would have been my father's ninetieth birthday.
You are so like him. Dark eyes. Kind. His artist hands.

Maggie, you keep calling to ask me
about Virginia Woolf. I don't really know
what a "position paper" is. "I'm intimidated, Mom."
Oh. I can picture you, two or three, standing by the dryer,
waiting for My Ducky Nightgown, My House Pants,
and (this, a T-shirt with silvery pastel stripes) My Sparkles.
"It's my body and you're not the boss of me."

Now *To the Lighthouse* is our
currency of conversation, a bridge.
"I want my title to be, 'Desire and Longing.'"
Perhaps you'll read Pritchett's essay on Woolf,
about her "Temperament." Useful word.
I'd feel silly saying this on the phone, but—
there's a tea I got downtown, a Darjeeling
called Margaret's Hope. Nearly every day, I drink some.

We're still getting deluged here.
The wind's picking up again,
and I'm thinking of that mare at Cypress Ridge,

how at four-thirty she began
her eleven-month journey to the gray foaling barn.
About nurture—long ago I wrote a poem,
not from the mother's point of view.
Here's the last stanza of "Good Milk":

> It's shocking when the heart
> Finds safe harbor and something clumsy there,
> As if to prove this difficult, prosaic art
> Entirely human. How maladroit and fine
> As stumbling on a swallow's nest,
> Or someone saying grace, or letting down tears
> Remembering love.

> Across these fields of wind,
> Mom

Spellbound

Together we climb the bell-wakened hill
finding what we did not know we had lost
the sound of water on tile the way stone
will take and absorb and reflect back light
our heels learning the shape of cobbles none
perfectly round Time warps and bends These
are not our ancestors yet they are
as if sprung unwilled from the earth
rebozo-wrapped Dusted and dyed with the past
they appear from walls webbed over with vine

They are not priests Hearing their strong singing
I made the sign of the cross and we saw
riding on *burros* unpoliced three kings
their garments richly bordered their skins all
the shadings of dark They came as the dusk
turned deep and women at the old laundry
were wringing the last water from their clothes
Tres magos burnoosed tossing sweets rode by
and mothers held up babies for a touch
in the corn-smelling air a sip of gold

We kept on walking my daughter and I
and did not observe their act of homage

and could not say if a halted star
shuddered in the sky We have become part
of the story the story part of us
By the next morning when the rooftop dogs
of San Miguel start barking in the high
cold at the Buena Vida *el gorrión*
weaves his song on the loom of this day while
we breathe in the tang of yeast dough rising

Waking to the Early Trees

Peeled off like citrus rind, my old work's gone.
I have entered a winter country:
the waning moon, torn, and the sky, celadon.
And there's more time to ponder, Who am I?
The house smells faintly of yesterday's lentil
soup, and the air outside, of peppercorns
scattered by rain, a pungent small hail.
At times I envy beasts their peacefulness.
Nuances of birdsong beside the creek:
Soon the wild pear, her roots in the bank side,
goes lightheaded. We could be sisters, I think,
whose pale new petals fledge our crackled wood.
　　　Penelope's bed, hewn from an olive,
　　　owned magic I believe in, still alive.

Muddy River Girl

Nothing like that now.
                    "At Cleveland Circle,"
I told the friend driving me back, "there was once a drinking
                                    trough":
a glimpse of horses, their tails swishing,
the oval basin overhung with willows. Part for the whole,
synecdoche of the forties (like the lumpy cars).
Earlier he'd asked, over tea,
"Do you ever find yourself thinking of your father?"
His look, getting off the trolley with his briefcase full.

From my old room I watch the rain,
its gray twigs slanting in the streetlamp's cone of light.
Night's falling. My mother tells time
by the maple tree across the road: its leaves turning,
fifty autumns, one side sheared by lightning.
I can see the scars. Somehow what remains,
the trunk and three or four huge branches, is enough—
tilting eastward to the morning sun.

I learned to swim in this water;
the Sagamore word for Brookline meant
Muddy River, these shallows dark as coffee.
I stand still for a moment, blinking, the damp wind
lifting my long skirt . . .

How will I explain my dreaming ways?
Whose roads I've trespassed on?
My names?
   Yes, *we shall gather*

the past eddying around us—
twelfth grade, eighth, backward-flowing to
my kindergarten at the John D. Runkle School, and
    beyond—
the hours and days coming to resemble a pomegranate,
pulpy and full of seeds, its pith
ordinary, even bitter. And the juice, divine.
The October evening soon takes on
a cloudy radiance, a nimbus.

Much later
I pull the curtains,
say goodnight to my father's picture,
and shake the coins still there in the china bank he gave me,
an elephant, rose pink, painted with sprigs
of clover. Broken and re-glued.
Hearing the rattle, my mother in new flannel pajamas
rolls up her green plaid sleeves.

Cherry Ripe, and Rag Bone

I

After betrayal, there is a need for clearance.
I came here from the closed chapel—the weave
of its windows in the dark, like tapestry—
to dispatch a snake
and ask forgiveness of the garden:

> the beds, dry
> the gladiolas leaning, to be staked
> an espaliered pear nearly choked with nasturtium.

Out of the deep Gulf,
sea-cry and a western wind
tug at this house
waking into the known shape of morning.
Clean sheets.

It's clear enough to see the Farallons,
bare island edge of what's visible:
Noonday Rock. A buoy, blinking. Birds—
puffin and auklet, the ashy storm petrel—
gatekeeping for the souls of the dead
who go there to dwell.
I feel them around me today

like spent blossoms snipped
from hydrangea or the buddleia's sweet blue horn.

A marmalade cat stalks field mice
in the high grass.
I try to be orderly,
seek advice from the English lady everybody asks,
How to resurrect a garden?

Cut back, wet well, and feed.

2

Uncoiling the hose,
filling (twice) the basin of a young pineapple quince—
two years until the tart, heavy fruit—
I find, by the south wall, a rusted horseshoe.

And remember London, that September:
clip-clopping; a wagon creaking along Clarendon Road;
the soot-blackened man calling out
"Rag Bone, Ra-a-ag Bone"
for castoffs to be taken away.
And myself a new bride, amazed,
hearing those footfalls echo
the ancient street-cry,
the waning of summer.

Will I ever learn not to fear the bare earth?
and let this autumn emptying imply
what life will come:
Early things. The days, lengthening.

"Cherry ripe, ripe, ripe"

Down I flew from the top flat
and paid half a crown for the punnet of Kentish Red
heaven: orchards teeming, the cherry fair,
girls dangling bright bunches over their ears.

3

Now on the windy mesa
blighted nectarine gives way to butterfly,
and a new lemon verbena
is opening into purple bloom.
Her hands unclench.

Every tree's been clipped, enough room between the branches
for a bird to slide through.
I walk this third of an acre one more time,
planning for autumn—

a load of mango mulch
and three fat tubs of food,

seaweed and diatom
sublimed to crumb. Gazelle-brown, clean.

Sundown light sifts through the cypresses. Pools of color
stand out, like rocks at low tide.
The forms of things reveal themselves:
a vase, a pincushion, a star.
And this garden, a boat
which sailor and crew have had to kedge
slowly, at a warp,
toward its mooring.

Inside, tonight
a few pink petals fall
from the Bolinas roses in their China jar
and lie, large and still fragrant,
on the dark wood.

Firstborn

For Ryan

1

From just this side of the sea wall
you can see the dolphins at play,
a fin or two, backs curving down.

The tide incoming, sanderlings
probe closer to the water's edge
than I am, walking toward Scripps Pier.

They are flocking creatures, all legs,
their tiny strides staying even
with the surf which foams at their toes.

2

On Sagebrush Road, this Fall sequence:
old pumpkins and the birth of twins,
their mother nursing them, head to head.

Outside near the new sod lawn
Ryan and I are planting bulbs
and baby-blue-eyes. Not yet two

he flings the crocuses, and it
delights him more than anything
to strew the bone meal in each hole.

3

The shore of winter: the gull's mouth,
open to a "V" when it cries.
Like the sanderlings, we try

to outrun the tide. It is in us.
In the garden, tilled; in this child.
When I thank him for helping me,

stretching out one palm he crows, *food* . . .
food, remembering the feel of bone.
His hand is a pink sea-star.

The Bird Hide

An observation structure;
a quiet place for watching birds.

Not all journeys are the same
straight line and a steady rhythm. The sun standing still
today, the creek creeping along
by pitcherfuls, we cross the uneven field, forward
and lateral like horses
leg-yielding, toward the small hut.

Sod roof and redwood slash invite us in. Screened
and shaded, we hear before we see:
the towhees' morning palaver; the sharp tap
of blue jay bills against the feeder; then
the hummingbirds' glittering green;
and one chipmunk flirting his bright stripes, sniffing up seed.

"At camp, my nickname was Chipmunk," you say.

In the half dark, we return to origins:
five years ago, that solar wind blowing us
far out on the mussel bed, where
old Purple Olive shells wash up. Each lavender husk

had a live hermit crab inside.
I told myself, ankle deep, sloshing through the cold salt,
"We didn't do this to stay dry."

Eighteen months since our marriage. Shelter.

It is noon now, and very warm.
In the tangle of trees above,
a snowy heron guards the nest. Her mate
heads out for the lagoon to fish.
By their gold slippers, their determined beaks, we know them.

Amber

How can we sleep for grief?
By counting our stock.

TOM STOPPARD, *ARCADIA*

At the edge of the Arden Forest, the farmhouse
where we used to stay . . .
It is changed here.
A darker trim. The rose beds gone,
turned into a laundry room. How few blackberries remain.

Just after sunrise, I've found my way back—
like a lover tracing the bones of a well-known body—
along the alleys: morning-gloried,
cat-streaked, vetch-lined, they connect the town.

What is memory, if not
some tincture of the mind,
our life, preserved in alleyways of amber?

Soon, when the rain spills her buckets of nails on our roof,
I will recall these sheep, just-clipped
polled Dorsets browsing in a warm wind.
A young filly prances free of her pen.

Now it all comes back,
that thicket of motherhood:

mazedly driving my daughter to school; trying
to smooth the syntax; the way she'd set me straight
as we listened to Redemption Song.
"Mom, it's supposed to be that way . . .
pirates, yes they rob I, sold I to the merchant ships . . ."

New moon, cradling an old one.

The morning planets are in bright
conjunction. Sometimes
thinking of this crabapple, the pollinator, saves me.
Ancient as a psalm, it climbs
uncanceled, dripping rosy beads.
Cats perch on the fence tops, like clouds.

A Sojourn

We returned with Indian summer
    and the pears of Jackson County sweet-naped
having reached maturity "3 For A Dollar" meant three pounds
    I learned and walked from that warm weather cloud
with the equinox traffic of wings overhead
    streaming toward the high grass on Grizzly Mountain
and crossed the tracks at West Hersey where the long trains
    still go through the whistle like a blown ram's horn
blaring down the Rogue Valley while the workmen
    on their break from Parsons Pine smoke and talk under
                           a frayed
tree of heaven It's near twilight when I pass the Helman house
    For Sale and some half-defunct sunflowers
next door By the light of a single bulb
    a farmer's sharpening his tools those scraped looking lambs
all shorn I'm thinking of our first visit here
    the way you called me *Dove who ventured outside*
at the Elizabethan theater your suede jacket fuzzy
    as staghorn sumac bark my vision blurring with tears
You could walk with me then only a small limp Maybe
    that woman in the play was right we do not give our hearts
they fly out from us and we are inclined to tumble after them
    May the past keep its secrets Sightless those concrete eagles

hunt nothing they glare at no one
    while the green of the year grows pale
like the rind of a honeydew melon this September moon
    cools herself in Ashland Creek where a screech owl
has come back to nest and redwood embraces black oak
    Now since the flood a bridge extends deeper into the park
whose corner is all shadow and silence We do not choose
    to go there nor take for granted
each few yards you struggle to walk
    the days of this week overlapping each other
like the scales of a fish We tear loaves for a brood of ducklings
    and one proud swan look out from our louvered room
on this sun-bleached garden its panoply of cats and on
                    our last
    full morning go for breakfast at the steamy "ABC"
dawdling over eggs The eleven-thirty freight whistles You kiss
          my hand

I Remember That Green Day

The morning star
had risen over the canyon by five
only the shadow of a cloud
creasing the mountain I left
some crumbs outside on the wooden tray
blue rosemary blossom tucked around it
before my long walk to the rocky gorge
where the great horned owls nest

Now in the embers of this dying year
the words of the great confession flicker
There is no health in us
Tonight as the rain descends and the wind's
perturbation wakes me
I am glad of my long walk
and of grace which comes unbidden
like the water

that gleamed from the mare's dark muzzle
as she lifted it dripping from her deep trough
or the crow I saw
inch his way along a branch of live oak
the burnt biscuit in his belly
eleven o'clock sunlight burnishing
his black coat
I remember that green day

Feast of Stephen

They've moved the stepping stones, torn out some vines
I'd planted, a decade, a family
ago. Our fence is built. Fresh sawdust winds
its trail around stout posts, spaced evenly
as the stars of Orion's belt. Fig tree
branches cast their shadows—veins or dark mapped
rivers—on red wood. Winter-shaggy cats
practice their descent. In a pale sun we
walk under mixed skies, the year curling back
on itself like a calla lily's white
envelope. A death, a birth, and all that
lies between: We struggle to inherit
    incarnation, board by board. At chill Yule
    here's food for the heart; for the spirit, fuel.

Little Black Rails

I have never seen it like this:
The end of Embarcadero—the marsh
a gray lake after last night's storm—
the water still rising,
starkening the sorrows of small animals.
Awake, the night heron cleaves
to his shrub. The muskrat swims slickly.
The mouse bobs along, a wine cork in plain view.
A peregrine waits to dive; in this new year
finding my footing, I am drawn to this tide, this danger.

A small crowd huddles in the mist. Crouched with them,
where dried gum plant and pickleweed tangle,
I can see two four-inch birds.
One darts toward the bay. On his dark back,
the spots I'd thought were water are his own
speckles of sea salt, or white pepper.
One comes toward me, a jewel on legs:
his onyx head; the nape, chestnut;
the body, lighter black—

nearly the slate-blue of juniper berries.
I am disarmed.
Little Black Rails on long toes in rain,

if you were any less rare, you would have
(as the Eskimos say of every loved child)
many names. Feather, pebble, shell—small things
take on large meaning. Amid the breakage, the dead stalk
of January . . . Imagine
having that wild pulse, that living shimmer.

This Rueful Moon

I

Cold as Mink Brook near my sister's, and boulder strewn,
the language of the Discharge Sheet has traveled home
                              with you
my mother, sent out after five days from the Beth Israel.

Condition: Walking; not Expired; not Other. Your heart rate
less wild, nor yet restored to normal rhythm,
you sleep downstairs in the small study

and take your meals from the same enameled tray
you'd bring our toast and jelly on—with sugared tea—
when we were home with colds, from school.

And unusual, this first morning, you remember
a dream: "I was putting on a sweater, when moths
started to fly out, and a woman from *The Atlantic*

(my father's old office, on 8 Arlington) said,
'Don't worry, we'll take care of it.'"

2

Between the nine-foot tides this month
a grebe dived straight
into December water deeper than its size
and opaque. Salt taste of pickleweed, of tears.

How ill all's here about my heart.
Wednesday, just hours since the electric jolt
to slow that dire knocking at your ribs,

uprooting the impatiens
(stubborn, half-killed by frost) I shook off the dirt,
made room for winter pansies, "Blue Beacon,"

and took the night flight.
The nurse, visiting, records your pulse:
seventy to seventy-five. Supper is baked cod; afterward
we watch the news. I am glad to have come.

3

So cold, the lock on the church door froze. I walk awhile
among the famous beech trees, whose dry seed pods,
four-pronged husks, gape open, their sweet nuts gone.

Now the slender leaf buds, furled, take comfort from
old bark—
ash-gray, color of this winter sky.
And the parched ground shall become a pool.

By noon you feel tired, telling me, "In one week
we'll get a minute and a half more light.
And I'd really like to have my mother's clock."

How many birds each year outlive
the poacher's boat? I think of egrets, cinnamon teal,
or mallard, turning soon for breeding, that violet-green.

Evening arrives at your west window; we look out:
a cat's tooth, a sickle blade to chop through frozen seas—
what a work of mercy this rueful moon is.

Anniversary

Here on this old volcano land snails coil to the left
    There has been a drought They are not now starved
                      for water
of another age the *bo* leaves dripping their green rain
    filling the storied garden the clefts of rare forked palms
The moon still new thickens An owl feather brushes by
    cloaked in dusk There is time We have not forgotten how
all night under the watchful eye of Venus the sea
    converses with interruptions and broken lines nor
what dry dark passages tunnel through the crater
    whose stairs ascending seaward open to the simple
truth of wind and the long Hawaiian wave spinning us
    into the center like a blue Cattleya orchid
On Kalia Road two ringed doves wade in the small streams
    and pools before they disappear Their violet throats hold
all the mauve complexities of dawn a lonely ship
    coming closer its one red light flashing Not allowed
to bring away *hala* root or the *quipo's* odd winged seed
    we are what we can touch the *bo* leaf shape of a tear
the sea's breathing forever over its sunken bone
    mild air on this leeward shore a hand drawn over skin
like wild fruit We awake in the peace of being known

It Snowed

last night in the high forest huge crystals
    lying on stumps and shake roofs I woke fearing
a wolverine the future my life a bone fractured twice
    and mended more than half gone
Climbing from the Happy Isles starting upward
    steeply till a patch of white frazzle-ice
turned me around I never got to the Emerald Pool
    Instead a warming met me on the bridge
precise blue Stellar's jays ruffling their dark crests
    losing their shyness in the sun
The wake-robin spills his blood by the river
    Winter dissolves her body
cascading over granite as I hope I will some day
    I am changing becoming part of the Vernal
Fall these fissures A water-ouzel
    running on the bottom with slate colored wings
half open I am not yet finished with singing

Charisma Longs for the Water

Her deep gouge healed, and the infection near the stifle
gone, she carries me willingly
along the trail at midday, in a fierce solstice light
that sears the oaks, that might set ablaze
the ears of jackrabbits or the straight silver
cheekpiece of her bridle. Barely six,

she knows the way to Alpine Creek, how to get up close
and stand parallel, while I nudge
the gate open with my crop. Shaking her black forelock,
impatient now, she paces down the leafy path
and wades right in among the minnows,
up to her wide Morgan barrel. Hearing
hooves strike wet stones, and the sucking noise she drinks with,

I am cooled, and think of the barn at night,
how its breath of sweet grass and new shavings
soothes the itch of loss; how muzzles lift
and nod, that softness just between the nostrils,
like a fresh peach; how the most fretful
mare will suddenly go peaceful when you rub her, there.

I Hear the Cricket Cry

Eight miles north of Salinas—
three weeks south of June—we take
a detour at Crazy Horse Road.
When it's hot and hazy like this,
the oaks nap, and their dreams unlock
the brown hillsides. All bodies
open in the summer time:
our hands grow sticky from its ink.
I become a garden lady
with a changeable tiger's-eye.

Too much rich grass, and the mare will
founder, the pulse in her fetlock
too strong. I get homesick; I weep
over dead umbels and vinca
immune to my dragonfly spells.
Every morning, one gray bird
hops into the overflow
from my watering and bathes.
There is no alertness like this
damp puffing-out of chest feathers.

When Mary Magdalene mistook
Jesus for the gardener
was she altogether wrong?

Forgiving, the hardest work
we have to do—you and I
touch it nightly. The moon thunders
past us, turning the brassy
sunflower blue-white. A sweet pea
folds her butterfly wing; she knows
these extremes of fury and love.
In the season of crickets
the heart is a tide, is a tree
whose great fronds lap my sleep.

Falling on Grass

Stumbling on melons, as I pass,
ensnared with flowers, I fall on grass.

ANDREW MARVELL, "THE GARDEN."

The house is sold; I take my leave. Not mine,
that room where I lay shipwrecked, sad thread
unwound from Love's bobbin. His eyes were stone.
Bee winter, when the hives cast out their dead.
Once I drew flowers, petal and leaf but no stem.
My teacher scolded, "You don't *have* to *breathe* . . ."
This March wind rioting through my garden;
Time's great beach; flatfish, thirsting, trawled by grief—
I've always liked odd company. Ten years
and a green health growing, here we all met:
hummingbird sucked Lenten rose, and lovers
spoke—seashells, bright bone the owl-limpet blessed.
    Still he'll scour our reef, his mark forgiven.
    Now I have been freed. An old flaw, shriven.

Light Arriving (The Strait of Georgia)

1

Yellow April: Time now to lay the sunflower seed
on its side in the warm greenhouse

earth, "And press down with your thumb" just so
in stages it happens, our parting from winter's body:

Out of the tenebrous station the train
juddered through Ballard Locks north, till

at Blaine midmorning I saw a great blue heron rise,
lift himself over the clamshell

border and veer toward White Rock—
then posted home my heavy black wool.

2

A silver canary, the seaplane
breasts Coal Harbor. The sun, moving downward, blinds

a Cyclops: the dredger's maw gapes wide—still the bird lands
safe. *Be not afeard, this isle is full.*

Here, five years ago my first small book was born.
By dusk I'm in the garden's faint

reek of smoke, old blackberry canes burning, hacked
to free the rhubarb, standing spindly red.

One taste of sorrel makes my mouth wince: sour-leaf, green
requiem for winter, pulled from this raised bed

where the dog, golden in her spring
coat, is nosing some carcass of crow or dank nest

or hidden selves (like the two white
trillium I notice later by the kitchen door).

3

Off Vesuvius Bay Road, turning, I step into
palomino light, the shady voices of Duck Creek

washing over silt and dulled gray stone, the lemon spathes
of skunk cabbage, flaring—they know

you do not have to die to get reborn. Above me
maple branches droop. Their yellow

flowers toss like forelocks of horses. Before the leaves,
before those wristed hands unfold,

everything awaits anointing;
inward, the pollen tube can hear the bee.

4

Not with the eye but with lateral line will a fish
sense location, a nearing—

Dawn, and the sky's peony. At the Indian Reserve
we discern the trail, rubbed tree root

and fallen trunk; spruce and madrone exhaling
their cool breath. I stand still. Dimmed

sunlight stipples the leather knapsack I've borrowed
from my friend who was so ill and now, it seems,

has healed. *O fools and slow of heart*—
somewhere out by Skull Island a canoe floats empty.

And these waters teem with food. Shoal-
deep, silver below and above, dark,

the oolichan approach their pierced horizon.
One day I will sleep silent and—all fin—

pass through those narrows: a candlefish; for that long
swimming home, transparent, like waves.

NOTES

"Neither Can the Floods Drown It": Cf. King James Bible, Solomon's
Song 8:7.

> Many waters cannot quench love,
> neither can the floods drown it.

"'Guadalupe Days'": *Ten Piedad:* Have mercy; *malecón:* breakwater.

"Spellbound": *rebozo:* shawl; *tres magos:* three magi; burnoosed: wear-
ing a hooded cloak; *gorrión:* sparrows; *Buena Vida:* good life.

"Waking to the Early Trees": Penelope's bed: With its significances of
faithfulness, lasting love, and restoration after loss, the bed of
Penelope is at the center of Book 23 of Homer's *Odyssey,* the
reunion of husband and wife. To reclaim her, the returning hero
must prove he know the bed's secret: it cannot be moved with-
out chopping through the still-living tree which comprises its
main bedpost.

"The Bird Hide": 1.1: Cf. Theodore Roethke's "Meditations of an Old
Woman": "All journeys, I think, are the same . . ."

"Feast of Stephen": Cf. old proverb, "Love your neighbor, yet pull
not down your fence."; Cf. *Oxford English Dictionary,* con-
cerning the word *fence:* sense 4. "That which serves as a defence
(a) Of persons: A bulwark."

"This Rueful Moon": "[H]ow ill all's here . . ." *Hamlet,* V, ii; "And
the parched ground . . ." Isaiah 35; "to chop . . . seas," This
metaphor is a variant of Franz Kafka's (roughly) "a poem is an
axe, to chop the frozen seas within."

"It Snowed": Wake-robin: In the United States, any of various species
of *Trillium,* including a rare species of burgundy hue.

"I Hear the Cricket Cry": The triplet here refers to the moment of
"intense recognition" (Denise Levertov, *Communion,* ed. David

Rosenberg) in the Book of John 20:1–16, when what had been feelings of isolation and despair are transformed, by a tender encounter, into hope: "Woman why weepest thou? Whom seekest thou? She, supposing him to be gardener, saith unto him, Sir, if thou hast borne him hence, tell me where thou hast laid him . . . Jesus saith unto her, Mary . . . she turneth and saith unto him, Master."

"Light Arriving (The Strait of Georgia)": "Be not afeard . . ." from Shakespeare's *The Tempest*, III, ii; "O fools . . . heart" from Luke 24 (King James version).